DIEGO

LIFE & LESSONS FROM MY CHRIST-CENTERED COMPANION

D J PAYNE

Publishing Coordinator – Sharon Kizziah-Holmes
Cover Design – Jaycee DeLorenzo, Sweet 'n Spicy Designs

INDIE
PUB
PRESS

Springfield, Missouri

ISBN -13: 978-1-964559-89-6

DEDICATION

To the compassionate veterinarians who take care of our pets when we don't know how. Each animal has their own personality, and yet the people we trust to care for them have my highest regard for the years they skillfully treat them, and during the final moments of love when we need them the most.

CONTENTS

ACKNOWLEDGMENTS

Recognition goes out to all that participated in the writing of this book, whether physically or emotionally. To my family and the way they have treated their own pets. To the animals under their charge that have helped all of us care for the canines and felines we've been blessed with all these decades.

INTRODUCTION

How many first graders are capable of performing an algebraic equation? How many 70-year-olds can run a marathon? A few of each I would imagine. And if we say we can't do something, we're probably right. On the other hand, if we think we can, we also are right. The simple trial, on our part, is trusting in God's ability to help us to see it through no matter the task. What do we do, where do we go? Eventually we may resolve this by saying, "God what's next?" It is within His power and means and desire for us to succeed; to succeed at what He finds is good and whole and meaningful for His people. Born with purpose, for a purpose. You are one of those people who He desires to succeed and to be fulfilled with all the beautiful wonders this life has to offer.

You've heard that timing is everything; the plans God has for us will be revealed in the right time, at the right place and in the right amounts so we're not overwhelmed, taken by surprise, or given too much to handle. **Proverbs 3:27** says God withheld knowledge from the people He was teaching because they wouldn't understand, or it was more than they could handle at that moment. Who's to say we are not in the same place as the ancient Israelites-not physically of course-but that we must mature over time to learn of God's ways and His desires for us. His will, will be done. Why not allow Him to direct our feet along a path already laid out, one that is secure and in the loving arms of the One who has our best interests at heart during the seasons of our lives, shaped just for us.

We'll have questions as to how this all works. Yet when do we ask the questions, knowing not what the answer is going to be, should be, or to where we are going, to whom should we turn for those answers? At some point we all think we are crystal clear as to where we're headed, what we want from our existence, who our friends should be, *how smart our parents finally are*, how much money we need to make, and on and on. If you're the least bit confused, then you are truly part of the masses who have wondered and wandered for a very long time with questions to which the answer has been placed squarely in front of us for over 2000 years. So, wouldn't it be easier if there was a roadmap to follow?

Something we could look to and say, "there's the way I should go, that's exactly what I should do!" And if this map existed for just such a purpose, where would you find it? Would you buy it, use it, and what would you pay for such a map? *Perhaps this map would cost a great deal, or nothing at all!* God has laid out before us a road map of His design. And we are central to that design; born on purpose, with and for a purpose possibly not yet known. A highway which may not be the smoothest of roads, but it does lead to places, people, and joys beyond anything we could ever imagine.

Where am I going with this?

Later in this book I and others will share experiences we've had relating to God's hand in our lives, through our pets. Yet this book is primarily about how the animals which occupy so much of our lives, time, attention, steal our hearts, and give back without expectation, truly reveal something about God's heart. So, even though 'Fluffy' routinely misses the litter box, or 'Fido' has a constant need to chew on our favorite pair of shoes, we find that we can't live without them-- and I believe that to be by design: His!

God's ability to design a companion for me or for you is not without great thought. All He does, He does for His children, and our response is to worship, love, and praise for the creation which engulfs us. As the Bible says, what father doesn't give his children the best gifts that he can with what he is able; **Matthew 7:11.**

So why wouldn't our Heavenly Father provide the best that even this life can't comprehend? Why are there millions of different kinds of birds, trees, fish, dogs, or cats in a multitude of colors and varieties; not only one kind of any particular thing, plant or animal? God desires to provide for us, help us wonder at His creation, appreciate and care for what He has placed in our charge, be those plants, animals, and each other from babies to the oldest and wisest among us.

He has a specific design to care for His children-young or old and promises to be there when we desire His attention. As each of us are not like the next person, all of us in His creation are designed with a specific purpose, and we serve to glorify Him in His kingdom.

I believe part of God's purpose, with each new baby born, is to staff His 'army' for the missions ahead. And with each new child He believes in our ability to carry out those missions; He still has hope for us as His people to perform, arm and save the people and animals He puts in our lives, whether that be many or few. He allows us to experience only what we are capable of handling with the trials set before us; for He knows our limits, yet expects us to reach beyond our normal boundaries, seek His help and use His best when we are at our least.

In praising Him for all He created around us I refer you to this verse from **Rev 4:11**…*You are worthy, our Lord and God, to receive glory and honor and power, because you created all things. It is by* *your will that they (*plants and animals*) exist and were created.*

As humans, we are His chosen race to enjoy this world and all its beauty. And this life is a marathon, not a sprint that we can casually glance at without noticing the wonders placed along our paths. What we also 'enjoy' is the free will to choose as we think best, and what a problem it can be if we don't choose to follow a path prescribed by the Creator of the universe. By listening and paying attention to the canine in my life I learned a great deal about the kind of life I should live that otherwise I would not have been privileged to. Please enjoy this reflection as I replay years of blessing known as *don Diego de la Payne*, or just simply, *Diego.*

1

STATE OF BEING

No doubt you picked up this book, or were given it, because you are a pet person. You are a lover of animals and one who sees the value of having a pet around the house to add to the excitement of your existence, lengthen your life with less stress, make new friends, add to the economy of your community by building a fence you otherwise would not, and someone who looks forward to vacuuming pet hair on a weekly or daily basis. Yes, there are ups and downs surrounding raising, coddling, caring, and *learning from your pet*. The last point is what this book is entirely about.

The above thought, to learn, is the reason for this reflection. From my own perspective and others, these great creatures, whether they be large in stature or small, can provide us with lessons to live our lives in a Christ-like fashion, if we only pay attention. And, as we proceed through this book, I will share episodes, not necessarily in chronological order, but in a way that shows the talents, compassion, and intelligence of one of my best friends, this side of Heaven: Diego. Looking into those big brown eyes, those same eyes can melt an iceberg to vapor and also tell me fido is always ready at the drop of a soccer ball, or Frisbie, to work off his daily rest, waiting for my arrival after being gone for the day. I believe a #5 soccer ball worked best for Diego. In the nine years he was with us, it is difficult to count the number of trips to the store to find his new best ball. And he knew when he had a new toy. Just the same as when we receive an unexpected gift and can't wait to be all over it.

One of Diego's daily routines was patrolling his property. It only seemed right that in order for all to go well during the day, the property should be a safe haven for everyone and everything inhabited there. We lived on an acre of land bordered by a fence (yes, the aforementioned fence) with neighbors on the east and west sides and a pasture to the south with *wildlife* in the pasture: the kind that eats all day and chews their cud when not eating. You may think these bovine intruders were of no consequence to anyone, but Diego had issues with them being all too close to our fence, snorting regularly "back off" my space. And this patrol was not a once-a-day event, oh no. It occurred morning and evening to ward off would-be creatures such as possums, raccoons, and a neighbor cat who dared to enter his domain.

Emotionally, a domestic dog exists in a kind of perpetual adolescence, a long summer twilight of play and napping and a happy routine in the company of dog parents who never age, and the dog who never lets them grow up. The scientific term for this Peter Pan state when adult dogs retain juvenile traits is "neoteny," and it can be one of many characteristics of canines as they age.

Happiness cannot be overrated when it refers to your pet, dogs in particular. You can go to the hardware store seven times on a Saturday, and each time you come home, it's like you just arrived from a long overseas trip. Glad beyond glad to wag and lick and head for the ball like it was the first time of the day. And this enthusiasm for "their person" brings the joy only a loving, caring, and compassionate pet can deliver.

Perhaps this is like a watchful God who cares for His children to secure them from the one *'prowling around like a lion looking for whom he can devour'* **1 Peter 5:8.** This roaming to patrol the property was not an ask of my pet, nor was he trained to provide this service, but out of duty and love he made certain that day and night, we were safe from all enemies. **2 Thessalonians 3:3** says it well: the *Lord is faithful, and he will strengthen*

you and protect you from the evil one. All of
Psalm 23 provides additional comfort and
assurance needed, along with **Deuteronomy 31:6:**
*Be strong and courageous. Do not be afraid or
terrified because of them, for the Lord your God
goes with you; he will never leave you nor forsake
you.*

And of course, while on patrol there were other, a
bit more dangerous, wildlife than the cows;
because there were coyotes in the area. A pack
lived not far from us (or at least they didn't sound
far away). But you can bet when they were in the
neighborhood, Diego was smart enough not to
engage a pack of hungry meat-eaters. Even though
he was half lab and half German shepherd, the
more timid side of his personality kicked in for
self-preservation; knowing that he had a greater
purpose for which he may not have even known
himself. So, while the coyotes are valuable and
serve their purpose, we can find them annoying or
troublesome. I believe while we   best leave the
coyotes to their happy frolicking or menacing,
Diego knew the value of a fellow creature's
importance on this planet. **Luke 12:6** & **Matthew
10:29** talk about how the sparrows are important to
God, *and not one falls that he doesn't know about.*
All God's creatures are important and play a role
to maintain balance in the universe.

Dogs are in many ways our mirror species. They

get sick and die like us, acquire arthritis and heart disease and, with many experiences of cancer, they too can grow frail and forgetful. And yet through treatments, medicine, and procedures, it's possible to extend their existence, possibly only for our benefit. There are conflicting theories as to why we would set up housekeeping with these carnivores. Possibly to begin the process of mutual domestication that confers survival instincts on both parties. Human and canine genes, shaped by the environment we share, evolve in lockstep. People with dogs sleep better. From our own experience, the nights are more restful, more efficient. We humans weigh less, and get more exercise than our dog-less peers. As I borrow a few words from an article from AARP[1] magazine dated January 2015, this burgeoning *dogoir* revolves around the basic idea in which a dog is foremost an instrument of personal growth: it exists to ease your anxieties, impart lessons about love and friendship, and teach us how to be better versions of ourselves.

Q: Self-evaluation and seeing traits or behaviors which you would like to change can be life-changing for the good. What do you see in yourself

---

[1] **AARP, the Magazine** *Our Dog Years,* written by David Dudley **Dec/Jan. 2014-15**

or your pet that reveals a difference you would like
to update, reform, make new?

2

CATS AND DOGS

MUTUAL FRIENDS

I've had the privilege over the years to reside with both cats and dogs from the time I was a very young lad to the present day. What I have learned, one of the many things I have retained, is dogs have owners, cats have staff. Fact of life, folks. One of my favorite felines was a calico named *Fluffy*, of course. How many thousands of Fluffys are out there? Who doesn't have a Fluffy if they have a cat long enough? She was a mouser, a bird-catcher, and, while a great lover of the outdoors, she also loved the indoors, with her people snuggling up beside her, waiting to be petted and pampered. Some cats are distant and would prefer it that way, yet they are valuable also to our well-being, and again, the ecosystem; they do their part to maintain nature's balance. ***Genesis 1:26*** reminds us *we are to have dominion over all the animals*, yet live side by side.

And while Adam spent a good deal of time naming them and caring for them in the original environment of Eden, the cat has evolved to remind us of who's really in charge in the house. It's possible they are more evolved than we may care to think. So, stick with me on this thought: independent but needy, and that's okay. All of us have the need to be dependent on someone else for thoughts, emotions, finances, intellectual stimulation, and on and on. While the feline loves to tout how "independent" they can be, they know where to find the milk and food. I believe an inherent reliance on what they know to be the secure source of their subsistence. If your cat hangs around, they know from where every perfect gift derives despite their occasional indifference to your pleading or suggestions. *Matthew 6:26* says the *birds of the air neither sow nor reap, but your father looks after them. Luke 12:24* echoes this sentiment: *The ravens don't need to plant or harvest or put food in the barns, yet God feeds them...*

As I said earlier, we, from Adam forward, have been given charge over all the beasts, great and small... to take care of them. And by doing so, we are served by multitudes of different animals at our disposal. Animals to plow the fields, animals to clear bugs from the air, ones to ride in an arena, to show off at the county fairs, for the simple pleasure of viewing from a distance, and to give us comfort and security. We belong to them for interaction, support, physical and emotional well-being, just as they belong to us. For instance, how many nursing home facilities have an adopted pet wandering the halls as the resident "therapist" to bring comfort, solace, or a listening ear without judgement or criticism. If our pets were paid an hourly wage for the therapy they provide, we would no doubt go broke. I very much like the following image, relating to it in many ways, and can see the depth of the appreciation this owner has for his dog.

I would not leave you behind for ANYTHING.

I will carry you over hard times like you have carried me through mine.

Q: We all have things that we've been charged with hold great responsibility on our part—to care for and nourish, to see they achieve their full potential. We all have dozens of things for which we're responsible. What is in your charge that needs your attention, concentration, a daily focus?

Luke 22:27 gives food for thought: *Who is greater, the one who receives or the one who serves.*

3

HOW DO CATS AND CANINES
MIX IT UP

While we're on the topic of cats and dogs, I can't stray far from the pair we had for quite some time known as Diego and Effie. Effie Fern Bigglesworth III. We weren't satisfied with simple one-name monikers, so we had to concoct these elaborate lengthy names. It was hard to put all of it on a name tag, so we didn't. Effie was the senior of the two, and she knew her sovereignty in the realm of her earthly kingdom. But she wasn't so sure how or where on the ladder of importance to place this new beast that came to be in our home once Diego made his presence known. At first, they were approximately the same size and weight, but as time passed, the lab/shepherd outweighed the feline a good ten to one

And yet, it didn't matter to either one. A mutual

respect was born. Not necessarily a friendship, but a launching of territorial boundaries punctuated by the passing of time to evaluate each other in this shared environment. A ton of fun to watch, for sure. Effie was a one-person cat. You know the type. I will let this person who feeds me also give me some lovin', while you, over there, on the other hand, deserve to serve as my scratching post. As I explained in the previous section, cats have their way of being indifferent as it suits them to please *or* not to please and this certainly begs the question of why they need to be so downright obstinate about certain things. However, Diego was determined to bring out the youngster in her. Picture the dog in play mode, head down and wagging his enormous tail enough to create a windstorm or clear the contents of any coffee table. This is how he would entice her to chase him down the hallway until, reaching a dead-end turn-around point the chaser became the chasee! I know for certain they were not in a fast pursuit to bring me pleasure, but how could it not. To hear the pounding of paws down the hallway, followed by a miniscule moment of silence, only to reverse itself in the other direction. I would anticipate this chase with a smile and think, if they only knew what joy it brought to our hearts.

God desires us to have pleasure from His creation and all that is in it. To bring us joy and contentment with all He has created for us, for our use. I saw Diego as the one who always had the other person or animal's best interest at heart. If I could add a noun to his lengthy name, and we had already labeled him with it, it would be *Service*. **Galations 5:13** commands us *through love we serve one another*. And without reservation, any expectation of reward, judgment, or fear of self-preservation, we are commanded to do just that. He, Diego, did and He, God, does that! A mouthful, I know, but take a few moments and digest this.

The pair, Effie and Diego, became the best of friends during the time they shared similar surroundings. Not until Diego and I went down the road on other adventures did the two of them part for good, not knowing they wouldn't see each other again. But, to their credit, they both went on to serve in the home and place where they were, bringing comfort and peace to their masters.

Another example of a kind heart and a willing spirit was the night we found a small white poodle cruising down the road in front of our house. No visible owner, with no tags but obviously a pampered house pet who got loose from the owners. He had apparently trudged through the weeds and was covered with dirt, briars and stickers, something this pooch was certainly not accustomed to. He came to us when called, however reluctantly, most likely taking comfort in the fact that someone was better than no one. As we took him in and introduced him to Diego, the poodle was trembling with fear for his life; absolutely terrified of this very large and dominant canine in a strange and foreign environment. And yet, compassion and gentleness were the traits on display for the new visitor from the senior canine resident. The two quickly bonded over some fresh water and food and settled in for the evening. They joined together for a night of rest in Diego's house, which was in the garage out of the weather, and out of the sight and sound of the local coyotes. He, the big brother, did his best to bring comfort to the new poodle in his life, not knowing this was to be a very brief visit. *Leviticus 19:33-34*: *When a foreigner resides among you in your land, do not mistreat them.* And from *Hebrews 13:2*: *Be sure to welcome strangers into your home.* Christ welcomes us no matter our state of being, where we are, who we are or our present situation.

It seemed odd to me, Diego would take in this stranger, welcome the smaller one into his own house and place without a whimper of jealousy, dominance, or the thought, 'am I being replaced by this thing'? Our Lord is like that. Without a node of hesitation, He welcomes us into the place prepared for us, whether it be here on Earth in a place suitable for us to do His work or our final home of rest at a time of His choosing. This little pooch was lost, afraid, and in fear of all that wasn't his normal and comfortable surroundings. The very wise and converted apostle Paul wrote on several occasions, and in particular **2 *Corinthians* 12:9**: *Your strength Lord is manifest, made best, when I am at my weakest.* **Glory be to the Lord our God!**

The pair, Effie and Diego, became the best of friends during the time they shared similar surroundings. Not until Diego and I went down the road on other adventures did the two of them part for good, not knowing they wouldn't see each other again. But, to their credit, they both went on to serve in the home and place where they were, bringing comfort and peace to their masters.

Q: With kindness and compassion, we gather with God's angels to sing His praises; this is where our heart needs to be. Who do you need to reach out to as a friend with a caring hand and compassionate heart today?

4

LEARNING

Always remain a student! Ever heard such a statement? Mostly from your elders or from those who have lived a tough life of sorts. People always want to tell you to live each day, each moment, as though it's the most important moment, one you'll never get back. Whether young or a bit on the *seasoned side*, we can learn and grow from those times and trials we experience, even those which are not our own. The following passage from Romans came in handy in a multitude of situations while penning this book, mostly because service doesn't come in just one flavor, but in a way when it's most needed by the recipient at a particular moment in space and time. ***Romans 12:6*** states *We are given different gifts according to His purpose to serve in different ways*. While we ponder this verse, let's get back to the thought of always learning, having a mind open to considering opinions that do not always coincide with our earthly whims, desires, and emotions.

Over the decades of animals in the house, I have discovered our pets often take ownership, or take on the psyche, traits, the emotional stability and characteristics of their owner. My own Diego enjoyed watching TV, playing ball in the backyard, camping, and singing along with me while I played the trumpet. He did so with dedication to the activity and the willingness to please, no matter what we did. But more than what he did, it was how he accomplished it. It seemed as though he did what he did out of a devotion to his nature, his breeding, the integration of his DNA from birth. In our lives, God gives us the free will to decide when and how we wish to participate in our own downfall. He goes along with our independent spirit because He sees the value of allowing us to make those mistakes and then find our way back to Him. Our pets are quite similar. They reflect our love with patience and the belief that we are good and true when we, in turn, trust Him to care for us. Take care of the animals, and they will take care of you, as Adam's charge was in the Garden of Eden. And in the book of *Job, Chapters 12 and 35*, we learn from those animals we choose to surround ourselves, realizing they are quite good teachers. And *how* they can teach, as they have already learned from, ingrained with knowledge from the master educator.

Job 12:7-10 encourages us to learn from the animals saying, *Animals and birds have wisdom to teach humans, and God directs all of His creatures.* Let's see now, whatever can I learn from something that I can't talk to? I must feed and water this creature every day and clean up after him. It seems to me he could learn a few things like how to pick up the stuff himself or at the very least, do his business in the same spot in the yard without me coaching him through this process. (Actually, Diego made regular use of one quadrant of the yard without any prompting, guidance, or coercion: making my job quite simple.) I could learn things such as *compassion* as demonstrated before, *service* without the expectation of a returned favor, *contentment* in my present state of being, the offering of myself without regrets, friendship to complete strangers (and other animals), and possibly the biggest and best of all, the forgiveness needed over and over, and over again! And this is the short list. Does this sound like anyone you may know or possibly need to pray for? There are countless parallels to connect my canine companion to Christ. It wasn't until after he had passed I realized that connection and the important role he played in my life. Thus again, the reason for writing this. I learned more than I could have imagined, having put into practice so much of what he taught me, and therefore I am better for knowing him.

Q: When you think you're done learning, you probably are. As the saying goes, whether you think you can or think you can't, you're right. Why not allow our experiences, friends, and our pets to teach us to be a force for good, for change? Learning should never cease, but be something we enjoy and grow from each day.

5

NEW PUP IN THE HOUSE

Did you know puppies are chick magnets? This is
what my son told me as   we're strolling through
Walmart loading up on needed supplies. We were
completely devoid of anything related to caring for
a newborn pup; it had been so long since I had one
in the house, or apartment, in this case. "Let me
hold him, Dad, cuz you know puppies are," well,
you get the point. If you want to make friends fast,
absolute strangers or not, bring your new pup into
the store and parade around like you're helpless
and in need of everything to properly care for this
new charge. Did you drive your pickup? Because,
that's what it will take to carry it all home with
you.

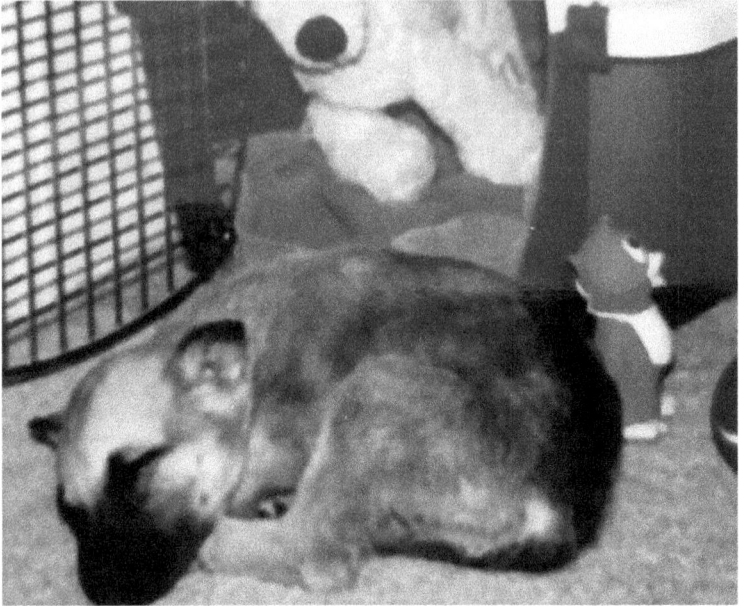

Who couldn't love a face like that? Half yellow Lab and half German shepherd. So, as he grew, he had this look like he could eat your lunch, until you provided the soccer ball, at which point he was your best friend for life. Rugged good looks with the personality of a teddy bear. More pictures to follow as we progress through this tail, uh, tale. He was the perfect guard dog, and appearances do count for something, but as your buddy, he would wag the tail and chase the ball until there was no daylight left. He did have those menacing shiny teeth, but only as the exterior to the passive and yet forever cuddly, nature of the Labrador retriever.

He knew his role: to protect and serve. Protect his people and property and serve without regard to his own safety. Case in point. For a period of time, we lived on an acre of land which was mostly fenced. The rain falls, and the grass grows, as is the normal course of things. And in between, rains with the grass nearing the height in which you could hide a small car, it was well past the time to mow. With an impending storm nearing our location, and no wet weather subsiding anytime soon, I was moving and mowing as fast as I could drive the mower. Diego was not happy with this activity. He could tell there was a storm in the area, and, according to him, I was oblivious to this fact. Every single time I would mow to the back of the yard, he would corral, attempting to herd me back to the house. And, once closer to the house, his effort seemed to be over until I ventured out farther, once again incurring the herd dog in him. Yes, I knew a storm was coming and wanted to complete the task at hand (hum, selfishly going my own way) and his only task was attempting to herd me to safety. How is this not like our Lord? Dogs can hear thunder much farther out than we humans are capable of detecting. They feel the drop of barometric pressure much more than we, sensing the impending storm and the imminent danger as they perceive it. And, while God already knows the storms that we will encounter, why would we not look to Him for guidance during those turbulent times we are destined to experience.

How are they, our pets, like our Savior? There is a

constant attempt to herd us in the direction we really should go, a direction which is truly the best choice for our lives. Granted, our pets are certainly not divine and have no powers of life or death, and yet, this simple act seems very Christ-like to me in that even though I was determined to go my own way (had to finish the yard), my four-legged protector had a better and safer plan for me. I just need to heed the warning signs and pay attention, period.

Even though we do so many things which are counter-productive, harmful to ourselves or others, even destructive to death, our Lord calls us back, attempts to herd us in the right direction, on the right path for our own well-being. Only a loving and selfless God can do that for you. *2 Timothy 4:18* brings us comfort when we hear how *the Lord will deliver me from every evil attack and will bring me safely to His heavenly Kingdom.* Guidance is available for those who ask. *Ask and it will be given you; seek and you will find; knock and it will be opened for you. Matthew 7:7-8*

Q: There are the four Cardinal points on a compass. And yet from the hub there are 360 degrees emanating out from the center. Once you move in any direction, you can even pick a half degree if you wish, move in your own misdirection, and veer off course pretty quick. It's always subtle at first, and then the snowball of missteps rolls down the hill very fast. We all need a nudge regularly to find the narrow path on which to trek. So, what path are you on that has too much of your attention?

6

HEALING

Backed by research and exhaustive study, it has been proven beneficial to have a pet in your midst for companionship, exercise, someone to hear our whining, and for *healing*. The physical benefits are obvious, but the most beneficial results come from the emotional well-being of having a pet in the house.

A long-term study from 1950 to 2019 revealed dog owners live longer than non-dog owners. This is from the journal *Circulation* in 2019. The benefit being greatest for those with a history of a heart attack. Research in the late 1970's by psychologists Langer and Rodin found that just having to care for a simple houseplant kept the elderly happier and alive longer. Just ask around a bit and you'll find hospitals, nursing homes, and recovery centers all use therapy dogs, and a few cats, to brighten the spirits and generate healing for even the seriously ill or infirm. Japan, however, has had a concern regarding allergic reactions to live/real pets. So, Paro, a robotic seal with artificial fur and a lovable face has been utilized to overcome depression in Asia, Europe, and in some parts of the United States. Another study from 2009 in the *Journal of Vascular and Interventional Neurology* looked at over 4000 people from a period of twenty years and for people who have dogs and cats had a decreased risk for death due to heart attack or stroke. So, while this information is less than exhaustive, a trip to your local shelter may be/should be in the cards for you, if you haven't already made that trip.

Having a pet close by has proven to me, and probably to you, just how the closeness and awareness of our animals can be a healing balm. From both the physical and the emotional needs that we have in our daily routines and on an occasional catastrophic basis. I'm not certain why catastrophe has to begin with C-A-T, but perhaps the two are related. Now, we've had cats in our house, and I don't discount the value of having a loving feline in our mix, but cats are sneaky about the issues/messes which may involve them. I'll leave it there for now. However, I am certain of the dogmatic (or principles to be incontrovertibly true) (hum, starts with D-O-G) ways our pets take care of us, often when we are at our lowest/weakest, emotional strainings. How do they know we are struggling, suffering, physically or emotionally, and are able to apply the correct measure of healing balm? They listen without passing judgment, take on our pain and make it theirs. Sound divinely familiar? There is no prescription for this medicine. Or is there? We are so proud to think that all our problems can be fixed if we pretend they will just go away. Or the idea around: 'it's my problem, I'll figure it out.' But paying close attention to our pets and the compassion they offer, we can surely find some sort of healing balm whether it be artificial, imaginary, or spiritual to solve our woes.

In the introduction, I talked about God giving us sufficient knowledge for the moment. Not too much and not too little so we could handle what lies before us. And when we get to the point of needing to be healed, we are charged with calling on our Father. For the times when we are in pain, our healing balm may be just a prayer away. Doesn't our God want to hear from us when we offer thanksgiving for the countless blessings, *and* in those other times when we are at our rope's end and can't see tomorrow for all the fog engulfing our lives? ***Psalm 145:1*** talks about *giving food in due season,* and *when they ask it will be provided.* I guess you can take the word 'food' to mean manna of some kind that sustains us physically, but I think there is a larger, more encompassing meaning to the word. All our needs, physical, emotional, spiritual, intellectual, and financial are met when we ask in His name with humble hearts and patient, open listening minds. As my son and I have learned through an interpretation based on **Matthew 7:7**: *Ask and it will be given to you; seek and you will find; knock and it will be opened to you.* Our loose interpretation breaks it down to this: *if you don't ask, you don't get!* Works for us.

Throughout the nine years Diego and I were together, we experienced many adventures. As it relates to our discussion above, we spent several weeks in New Mexico building houses for Habitat for Humanity, an incredible organization designed for those truly in need of good housing. The two of us were our own best companions, except for the rest of the building crew. We would take a good many walks, exploring the local landscape and enjoying the solitude of no conversation but healing from what were long and lonely times. Comfort just being together, thoughts, prayers, and companionship. God was there through all of it. And there were times I would play my horn, my trumpet, in the motorhome which prompted a howling sing-along. I knew or thought I knew he approved. Thank you, my trusted non-judging friend!

Q: *Ecclesiastes 4* talks about two being better than one: *better return on your efforts, and one can* *help the other if they fall.* It goes on to say *"a cord of three is not quickly broken." It matters not who or what your second is;* just make certain the third member of your party is strong enough to pick up both of you when you fall (and you will). Who are the members of your team?

7

To Protect and Serve

So, where have you seen the above words before? On the side of every police car in America. I don't believe Diego could read English, or at least I don't think he could. But I will admit nature endowed him with the right and responsibility to protect, the German shepherd part anyway. The Lab side of him simply wanted to love everyone. And he was a spectacular example of both. One of my favorite times was watching him play with the propane delivery man. Seems innocent enough, but the notion that a stranger would be invading his property did not sit well with the 90 lb canine. So, once I explained in dog terms why this man was here, what he was doing, and the benefit we would derive from his visit providing a source for heat and cooking, he tolerated my answer. He looked forward to the visit, and a soccer ball game would ensue. Diego would immediately charge for his ball and wait impatiently for the man to make the connection to the tank, then the fun could commence. And for the time during which the propane would flow, this delivery man and the beast of the yard would have a terrific time sharing a moment special to both.

This example of protect first, play second makes me feel we have a loving God who wants the same for us: protection from all unknowns and un-familiars until we can trust and believe in our fellow man. Then, as we build rapport and offer ourselves in the relationship of trust, we can let down our guard and believe in the beauty of those relationships with unwavering comfort.

From *John 12:26*, we learn if people have the servant's attitude, our Father will honor those who serve others in love and kindness. It's not at all difficult to see the joy from both the propane delivery man and Diego brought to each other during the brief soccer game. I'm not sure who was serving who more. What I do know is that with each return to fill the propane, Diego did not have to go through the introduction process again. He never forgot a face or a friendly smile, or, in this case, a playful kick of the ball.

Friendship for those he barely knew was an ongoing and beloved trait to which he displayed during the nine years of his life. A short time, even for a dog, stemming from complications in which we'll talk about later. A trust offered to others and built out of his nature, not something I instilled, but a God-given talent endeared him to all he met. Even during the last few moments of his life, "A big heart, this one," the vet said.

Psalm 121: 7-8; *The Lord will keep you from all harm, he will watch over your life; the Lord will watch over your coming and going both now and forevermore.*

To protect someone from imminent physical danger is one form of safeguarding, and yet to protect a loved one's heart from certain pain and suffering of emotional loss may be an even greater threat. More to come on the subject in a later chapter.

Service is something our pets provide without the need to be compensated; *John 12:26*. Now, for you cat owners, I understand the saying which goes, dogs have owners and cats have staff, this "providing" thing may seem out of reach for the household feline. But think for a moment how much comfort and reassurance our pets, including the beloved felines, horses, goats, milk cows, and all, bring to us. Without getting tied up with statistics, it is proven pet owners live longer, are more content and find solace and sometimes enjoy conversations with the family pet. And while the pet doesn't really ask for anything, our job is to provide them with an abundance of good food, care, toys to entertain, and our time, which they and us find really matters the most.

Don't you suppose the beagle, bloodhound, or spaniel would prefer being out in the woods chasing down a scent rather than curled up next to us on the couch, meeting our needs as opposed to theirs? How about the Shepherd Australian, German, or other nationality who would be more inclined to be in the field, barn lot, or somewhere he is able to herd something, anything! Working dogs have been bred to work, hunting dogs to hunt, and the list goes on. But, thankfully, they choose to be in service when and where we need them, when it's convenient for us, and mostly on our schedule, not theirs. Yes, we do have a patient God. But He is a jealous God, wanting our worship and commitment. But what he does offer us is the ability to need him, as we need our pets for comfort, security, companionship, conversation (don't tell me you don't talk to them). All of these we have in Him who gave us the right to love freely and serve each other as our four-legged friends choose to serve us without expectation.

My opinion once again, but I believe the *opportunities*, as I might call it here, and/or *tragedies*, that befall us, put those in our path either near or far placing us in a prime location to serve as eagerly as we have been served. Remember, there is nothing in our path that God can't equip us to handle, with wisdom, kindness, energy, and a discerning mind.

Q: The feeling of security in a relationship can mean unconditional love and friendship; respect with complete confidence that your partner is there for you always, and not just sometimes. Did you know your struggles and fears are not your own to bear? Find your peace and comfort in the One who created you. What struggle are you attempting to carry on your own that needs to go to God, your partner, so He can serve and protect?

8

GOOD LOOKS AIN'T EVERYTHING

Did I tell you he was one good-looking dog? Well, I'm about to repeat myself. The family from which we received Diego was our third visit on a day to find a pet. The others had sold out, most likely because they were all free puppies. Timing has a way of knowing when to rise to the surface for our benefit, whether we know it or not. This timing, being the third home we had visited was not a fluke or a chance happening. *I was destined for this animal and I believe he for me. It was a partnership planned long before we arrived at the house.* A couple of pups were left and, even though I was in the process of moving to an apartment, I needed a companion to fill the time and void. It became a matter of introducing ourselves to the prospective pup, coming to a meeting of the minds, but mostly just because he was such a cute ball of fluff, we couldn't say no.

So, off to Walmart we went, looking for supplies for our new-found friend.

What a handsome pup he was! Huge brown eyes and that golden coat made for a look that was irresistible. His temperament was about 80 percent lab, 20 percent shepherd. And yet when it came time to please, serve, or play, he was 100 percent puppy. He could find a variety of ways to make it fun: from walks in the country, assisting with a backyard volleyball game (he didn't know the ball in the game wasn't his), to chasing and being chased by the cat a 10th his size, back and forth in the house.

I know you've witnessed people who seem to have the capacity to serve tirelessly, with a smile no less. Where are they grounded that such a process can begin, how does it happen, and can we take what we learn from our pets and put it into practice with what God expects us to do for our fellow humans?

Yes, the most beautiful coat of fur I've ever seen; truly an unusual look for a German shepherd, "and he's part yellow lab also?" As he grew, he retained those rugged good looks and yet took it all in stride without conceit or bias. His powerful body galloped across the yard in hot pursuit of the soccer ball was truly an impressive feat of strength and grace. However, I don't think the stray cat wandering into our lives and across the wrong yard felt the same.

On a typical spring day in an otherwise routine course of things, a yellowish cat I hadn't seen before, and certainly will never see again, appeared in the backyard. As I was looking out the back window, I happened to pick up the chase already in progress. Diego had intercepted the cat mid-yard and was in blistering pursuit. I mean, this was his yard, and he was simply protecting his domain. The flavor of the chase did not have the same look and feel about it as he and Effie used to exchange. And as I describe it, it was over in a flash, far quicker than I can relate it here. From mid-yard, they were flying low to the west. And, on the west side of the yard there is a four-foot-tall wooden picket fence…and at the pace they were traveling I thought there was no way they would be able to halt before slamming into it. Oh, me of little faith. About ten feet from the fence the cat launched itself onto the top rung and cleared it, just as Diego came to a screeching halt, nose to fence, no doubt scowling at the intruder, nevermore to be seen in this neck of the woods. Nope, never saw him return. "My yard," he says, "safe for all once again!"

Kind of like the young shepherd boy, David, whom Samuel anointed to be the King of Israel, not based on looks alone as we humans often do. As you may remember, Jesse had many sons far more handsome, rugged, and stately appearing than David, but God chose him based on the heart of the one who would rule fairly and with compassion. *1 Samuel 16:7* says it this way, *Do not consider his appearance or his height, the Lord does not look at people the same way as humans do.*

Q: So, while Diego was a great-looking canine, it's his heart which forces me to remember him, learn from him, and journal about him. What can you see in your pet that reminds you to learn of the unconditional love poured out for us without merit or worthiness on our part?

9

RESPECT

Don't you secretly, just a little, wish your dog would "do his business" in someone else's yard? To have your place free and clear of distractions which cause the kids to get messy, or things could end up on their shoes, getting tracked into the house on the carpet. Oh yeah, nasty stuff. And not everyone will notice or be the one responsible for cleaning up. Thus, having a neighbor's yard seems like a great option, until of course, the neighbor finds out who's been messing in their yard. "Oops, sorry, it won't happen again!" Leaving it somewhere else would keep you from having to pick up after him all the time in your own place. Yes, I know when a dog has got to go, he's got to go. Picking and choosing the appropriate times for this activity are not of your choice; it happens when it happens. Seems like a dirty subject to bring up, yet this pup of mine knew his place and his time for all sorts of activities.

As a side note, yet related, I was asked to remove myself from a lady's backyard one day (not because I did the "business") but a home adjacent to a fairway on a golf course; because she claimed I had no right to have my ball land in her yard. And, scolded I was, "if I couldn't keep the ball in the fairway, I should take more lessons!" More lessons are good and useful for a great number of things, including playing better golf. I reflected on what I wanted to say in retort and yet simply picked up the ball, said thank you for the advice, and returned to the fairway. Certain folks you just can't reason with; I prayed for her. And besides, even the pros hit out of bounds occasionally. Just watch any golf tournament on any given weekend and you'll see it happen. Apparently, I didn't have the correct level of respect for this lady's yard. Life goes on.

So, where does this above story take us, and why is it included in this manuscript about dogs, other pets, and their behavior? As the title of this chapter indicates, it's about the respect we offer other people, things, animals, and the love we show even when we're not asked. Do we show others courtesy because we're supposed to, expect a reward for doing so, or simply because it's the right way to behave? Why honor the wishes of those we may not even know, or why do we help when not asked? Do we want a reward, possibly a monument erected on our behalf illustrating the kindness and immense generosities of our heart for the goodness we seemingly demonstrate toward mankind? The long and short of it is, do it as it has been done for you; just because! *From approval, not for approval*, is a teaser and a topic for later.

Recently I heard a message that pertained to the subject of approval and why we seek it. Is it for the notoriety or recognition by our fellow man? Service can be a good thing when done for the right reason. The respect we shower upon others is not because they deserve it but because it's what our Lord would have us do, even to those in our minds who haven't earned it. And it's a tough principle to swallow.

Philippians 2:3 says it this way, *Do nothing from selfish ambition or conceit, but in humility count others more significant than yourself.* Being humble, now there's a challenge. This is the part of what brings me back to my pup. God must have known I was a lousy trainer, or he was training the dog to guide me, because He installed a high degree of respect in my dog for other people's property. For example, hypothetically, if Diego could hit a golf ball, he would have known to hit only as far as he could to keep it in the fairway, not drifting right or left with the possibility of irritating someone. Similarly, when we went for walks, he would hold it until arriving back home and then find his spot in the yard to finish his business. It was only much later in his life he would have some difficulty finishing an entire walk without the health struggles which eventually took him. My firm belief is that, *if we pay attention, we are meant to learn from all creatures*. God cares for us and, while He has given us domain over everything created, His plan is to have us manage this creation to the best of our ability, learning all the way, and the ways He would have us treat others. *1 Peter 2:17* says, *Show proper respect to everyone, love the family of believers, respect God and honor the authorities.*

Q: Respect originates and is fostered by God. From *Isaiah, Respect is the permanent state of God.* Some other common synonyms for the same are admiration, esteem, and regard. We are all worthy in His sight, including those who you doubt deserve it. And yet today, who among you could use your admiration, esteem, and respect?

10

TRUST

A long time ago in a land far, far away... Well, maybe not *so* far away, but something I learned from ages past has served me quite well to this day: find a good dentist and trust them to do what they're supposed to do. A good car mechanic is truly irreplaceable, and cutting your own hair might have been cute when you were seven, but not now and not forevermore. Do I absolutely know without a shred of doubt that my barber is going to give me the haircut I need, not just what I want, but a cut where it doesn't look like a cut; just a re-shape from the previous day of shagginess? If I am terribly nervous about it, I should not even get out of bed to fulfill the appointment and face the day full of uncertainty and peril without knowing for sure what's about to happen throughout that particular day of events. But we do venture forth at supposed great peril, and why do we?

Trust is one of those topics I believe can be a weekend seminar with a knowledgeable outsider flown in from somewhere. He/she to dazzle and impress us with thoughts of uplifting revelations and behavior-altering enneagrams to refocus our energies and all of our thoughts toward letting go; but let go to whom or what or where? *Trust involves the realization that someone else may have a better plan than we do.* And if that is the case, who would the master planner be; what's the design for my life, and when do I pick it up and run with it? Being on the right path may be my mind set; but maybe my mind is a little foggy today and the morning didn't clear it as I had hoped or thought it ought to for these high-level decisions (like barber appointments).

As we are talking about changing paths, a verse from one of Solomon's books comes to mind: **Proverbs 3:5,** *Trust in the Lord with all your heart, and do not lean on your own understanding.* Because my own understanding is clouded with doubts, fear of failing, and the fear of what others may think of my ideas, I'm in a compromised version of what's best for me. I have a constantly changing mind as to what is truly the best path. Our pets, the animals God has charged us with, rely on us for their daily care and feeding, trusting us implicitly. They give their lives over to us without reservation or thought about what will happen tomorrow, next week, next year, or the next minute. My daughter has been in the horse business for quite some time, and I have witnessed her take a horse from the warmth and comfort of a stable to 10-below wind chills and snowing conditions to the outside pasture, with the horse simply following along without hesitation, resistance, or complaint. Trust is what they do! In my early days, we had a rat terrier named Stormy who was uprooted from city life to the open farm environment. He took to it quite well and found himself in a role as a great mouser in the grain bins. Being well suited to clear the pests and rodents which inhabited the barn where the corn was stored, he trusted us with this big move for him and made the best of his new environment.

Learning to trust, as our four-legged friends do, is a lesson we cannot afford to miss!

When I headed for New Mexico to assist with the building of houses for Habitat for Humanity, Diego knew not where he was going or whether he would ever be home to his safe and fenced haven. But he trusted and placed his belief in my ability to lead and provide for him. Life goes full circle, doesn't it: birth and infancy until death's door when we're feeble and can't care for ourselves; so we are in need of trusting others for our well-being/survival. On our trip to the Southwest, we spent many months on the road in the very used thirty-four-foot-long motorhome, and later that same summer, I ended up working for the Missouri Department of Natural Resources as a campground host. Part of the best spring and summer of my life: simple and without worry about politics, a job, or where the next meal would come. Just the dog and me. Sounds like there could be a country tune in there somewhere.

And if they, our four-legged companions, can trust us with the imperfect knowledge and limited skills we possess, how much more should we trust our Creator, Father and Giver of every perfect gift. Not an easy task but one where we can reap huge rewards. The first part of this next verse demonstrates in a small way how our pets feel about us. *1 John 4:18: There is no fear in love, but perfect love casts out fear.* He, Diego, had no clue where we were headed or the adventures we would experience for the next six months prior to his passing, but oh those times we had and the memories, the lessons I've learned; those will stay with me forever.

Psalm 37:5: Commit your way to the Lord; trust in him, and he will act. It doesn't say, if you can afford it, feel like it, or even if you feel you really need it today. It doesn't say give up everything you have or own, or you need to find yourself prior to joining *the team*. The concept seems simple, but putting it into practice can be so difficult. As I have discovered, living within the law is a better and much simpler place to be. There is freedom within God's law. Kind of like a four-year-old knowing what the boundaries are, where those fences (figurative or literal) are. They grow up respectful of the adults who lead them on the path they should follow.

An example might be thus: the law can be liberating. The first car I was allowed to drive was a hand-me-down from my parents, in good shape and modestly clean. Not the hot rod I had hoped for all along, or the super-slick wow-factor ride as I cruised main street in my hometown, but I got used to it quickly. As a more seasoned driver, I appreciate getting to my next location intact and without worry that local law enforcement will be waiting for me just around the next bend. And for my next road trip, or just the trip to the grocery store, you can bank on the fact I will not receive a speeding ticket, don't have to look over my shoulder for the locals, or even be concerned about road rage from the other traffic.

As with life, if I am living within God's law, obeying the precepts that he has for me, there are no worries about how or when I'm literally or figuratively going to *get there*. And the traffic, well, it may be passing me on a regular basis as if I'm in the wrong or misguided lane while the other motorists are asking the question, "Why can't you keep up with us?" Doesn't life imitate driving to a degree? If we're not going with the flow, there has to be something wrong with us, my methods, plans, me? See the parallel with this verse from **Psalm 20:7**: *Some trust in chariots,* (fast cars), *and some in horses, but we trust in the name of the Lord, our God.* Again, if the animals can trust us with the imperfect knowledge we possess, **how much more should we trust our Creator, Father, and Giver of every perfect gift on this planet**.

There are dozens of scripture readings which point us to the encouragement about trust, belief, and giving over to God the worries we have with everyday life. Over 90 percent of things we worry about we cannot do anything about. So, turn it over to the one who can and repeat this verse (to yourself) on a regular basis; **Psalm 46:10**: *Be still and know that I am God.* And now from the New Testament; **Hebrews 13:8**: *Jesus Christ is the same yesterday, today and forever.* Truly, the one and only we can count on!

It is my belief with dogs, not so much for cats, have the herding instinct. If you, as the human, are outside in the rain, woe be it for you 'cuz apparently, according to the feline queen of the castle, you just ain't bright enough to come in out of it! Where we were in the house mattered to

Diego because, as his people, if we were not in the same room, it was a real issue and needed to be remedied without delay. He would spend whatever time it took to herd us to the same location, that being within the same room, and then and only then could he settle and be comfortable for the night. I have recently learned a few things about a dog's character which I was completely unaware of. They are quite concerned with storms, loud bangs (such as those which come from fireworks), and the change in barometric pressure, as witnessed one afternoon while mowing the lawn.

As mentioned earlier, dogs are capable of hearing thunder much farther out than us humans can detect. They feel the drop of barometric pressure much more than we, sensing the impending storm and the imminent danger as they perceive it. Our pets are often so much like our Savior, attempting to herd us in the direction on the path we really should be following. Granted, our pets are certainly not divine and have no powers of life or death, but this simple act seems quite Christ-like to me. Even though I am often determined to go my own way, my four-legged protector, and my Lord, have a better and safer plan for me. I just need to heed the warning signs and give attention where it's due. *Trust.* It's what it's all about.

Q: Trust is defined as the firm belief in the

reliability, truth, ability, or strength of someone or something. The concept of letting go and letting God lead our direction is difficult for us humans, often thinking we know the right path. Remarkably, He can make good out of any situation, if we listen, and do. What you choose may be on you, but believing God can move your feet for the best outcome is ultimately the better, safer path. Allow Him to answer those tough questions when you have no place, no one, or nothing to turn to.

11

ACCUMULATING WEALTH

Dollars, Rubles, Yen, Bit coin, artwork, land, cars, cattle, or dog bones. What is your desire to acquire, and how much is enough? Does having a large family with lots of grandkid's appeal to you, (only if they don't stay over every other weekend)? Is it regular, *really nice* vacations, (we're not talking about day trips to the local fish hatchery to fill that bucket of memories, or is it the *look at where I've been* kind of trip)? What is materially important to you? It's okay if you need some time to make a list; I'll be here... Maybe it's being in charge, having command of your kingdom that stirs your soul and fills the bucket. But the problem with control, and most of the items above is, we can never have enough to satisfy our thirst. The temptation is if I have more, then I should have even more. I think there are multiple definitions for *wealth*, *riches*, and *success*. Each one can be defined as the situation fits. Being *rich* may indicate I have a lot of stuff, collections way beyond what the Joneses may have, but that doesn't necessarily make me happy, content or successful.

For Diego, the value he put into life wasn't about the things he surrounded himself with as much as the people who surrounded him. Security, comfort, health, friends, contentment, simplicity, moments together with close friends, and relationships, to name a few, were really the focus of Diego's existence. Security came in the form of having the safe haven away from the coyotes, and shelter from the weather in an indoor doghouse that accommodated him with a heated floor to ward off the winter's chill. His comfort came in many forms: a routine he could perform daily, morning and evening patrol and familiar items on which to chew, which brings me to convey this next point.

After the loved one is gone, you begin to realize and see things of the physical and intellectual nature that were not apparent when the person/animal was alive. 'Taking it for granted' is a phrase we often hear after something/someone has passed. Or maybe it's a job, possibly a possession which we held dear that is now gone. As a young pup, he would find things in which I had some association, things I had touched. Might have been a shoe, possibly a tool from the garage having some kind of handle, a pillow from the couch…you may know where I'm headed with this one. Yes, he would find the need to chew on these items, and while it became annoying to find stuffing all over the place, never to find my shoe, or to reach for the tool only to find it mangled, I took a different angle in approaching this frustration. Just maybe, maybe he was taking comfort, finding familiarity in the things which meant something to him. He didn't occupy himself with items that belonged to my wife, and I found it odd. So, consider this from a slightly different direction: you could make the case that he was *honoring me* by choosing those things I was associated with. None of those things were irreplaceable. None of those items were really all important to anyone but him, but his need to be comforted by what he deemed necessary to fill a void, bring solace, bring a sense of peace to his life. So, I don't know whether the puppy in Diego wore off and so did the need to comfort himself with items he found, or if he found comfort and ultimately the security with the passage of time, knowing where his people were, he was truly at home, home sweet home for him.

A dog's sense of smell is keen, to the tune of 100 times better than us humans. The friendly woodland bear tops the list at around 300 times more sensitive than humans. So, if you're in their territory, they will know it long before you do and have a plan for your existence, or not, in their environment. Dogs fall in the list at #5 out of the top twelve mentioned in an article from the journal, *Our Endangered World*, dated August 18, 2022. Animals survive in large part based on their sense of smell; fight or flight is bred into them, animals of all types. Fish even smell under water, for real!

We base our daily routines on a multitude of senses provided for us. Various passages encourage us to use all the senses we are given, to study and appreciate His teachings. For example: **John 10:27** says, *my sheep hear my voice, and I know them, and they follow me.* From **Psalm 119:18** says, *open my eyes, that I may see Wondrous things from Your law.* Also, from **Psalm 34:8** it says, *Taste and see that the LORD is good.* All of these references use what our human minds can comprehend to find purpose, safety, and understanding with the Lord. These are obviously figurative interpretations of how best to use our senses, but His illustrations are on our level so that we benefit. While our sense of smell or sight, and hearing may begin to fail us over the years, we learn to compensate by utilizing the other senses we're blessed with.

For a few decades now, I have worked around horses and the stables which house them. I've become a bit desensitized to the odors of the horse barn, the aroma which hits you well before arriving at the stable. It's all in what you get accustomed to, right? We rely on the animals around us to warn and prep us for the dangers and opportunities ahead. Staying within the realm of equestrian circles, my daughter's passion for horses has been constant for the past twenty-five years. Horses have a highly developed sense of smell that's more acute than us humans, but not as sharp as a dogs. Their sense of smell is important for their survival. Horses can identify medicine in their feed, even when it's masked with treats. They can also distinguish between different varieties of apples. Horses can use their sense of smell to avoid predators. For example, a stallion might detect the faint scent of a cougar and move his herd to safety. While my duties involve many different tasks, through experience and years of nurturing/training, I have become one of the best, and cheapest, stall muckers she has found.

For women, it is said *security* is their number one most important factor in finding and being with their mate. When considering *accumulating wealth and value*, what do you place at the top of your list, your measure of a reward that satisfies, the things that bring you happiness? We can learn a great many lessons from our four-legged friends by placing value in things which cannot be purchased with any form of currency but contain the essence of people and pets we love and cherish.

1 Timothy 6:17-18 states, *command those who are rich* (with many possessions) *in this world not to be arrogant nor to place their hope in wealth, which is so uncertain, but to put their hopes in God, who richly provides us with everything for our enjoyment.* Oh, how difficult it is to turn off the desire to possess and just say, 'more of you God, less of me.' Many times, throughout the Bible, we are told not to worry about what we'll eat or wear, but to focus heavenward and all of that stuff will be provided. It's a daily struggle, to walk in a race with the rats to just make ends meet, let alone accomplish the feeling that we've forged ahead somehow. And yet our pets provide a guiding light if we will just pause long enough to see how they look at life. I've never had an animal, small or large, holding up a sign, scratching out a message in the dirt, or verbally speaking to me like Balaam's donkey (one of three animals in the Bible), and asked, Where's my next meal coming from? *It's trust folks!* If they can do it, we can too, and there's great value, great wealth in letting go and letting God!

Wealth may define for me the ability to appreciate what I have and hold dear, and *success*, I believe, is achieved by helping others accomplish their goals and what is important to them. In a recent message heard on a Sunday morning, the preacher talked about the lies we tell ourselves or others tell us, and the unfortunate part is when we begin to believe what we hear and adopt a destructive attitude. The first of five lies is, *I am what I have.* So, sometimes we need to believe that in order to be *someone*, I have to a lot of stuff. Seriously? Not sure what your definition for wealth is, but for me, knowing what I have and appreciating from where it came makes me truly wealthy and wise.

Q: Rarely do we take the time to reflect and give thanks for the wealth provided us. I mean, there is of course, one day in November—isn't that enough? More time spent with the attitude of gratitude, and we'll spend more time thankful for what we have and not yearning for what we don't. Comparing ourselves to what others have is not healthy. You and your situation are unique and special to the One who created you. Why not give Him the credit for creating such a wonderful person? What are you grateful for today, about yourself or others? As time passes, we all have things that mean something to us from someone who went before us. Give thanks for those lessons learned and respond.

12

THE DREADED DOG PARK & DUSTY SANDALS

When my kids were young, together with their and our friends, we enjoyed spending time and would plan a day to *get together*. It doesn't seem so archaic to say it in that fashion, until you hear we now are having *playdates*. The Oxford dictionary says it's two words, so, we're going with that.

How many cities have a place for a playdate to include your dog? As of this writing, there are 774 dog parks in America. I think it's now one measure of the quality of a city, to have bike trails and dog parks. Nothing against them, but if the target keeps moving on how we evaluate where we live or the quality of life, how do we ever hit it? In **Hebrews 13:8**, it says, *Jesus Christ is the same yesterday, today and forever.* Thank God that's a target which never moves!

A town we lived in several years ago had a very large and nice dog park at one of the major park settings. They did a marvelous job of accommodating people and pets in this environment. There was a large zoo, all kinds of ball parks, a rose garden, picnic shelters, and playgrounds for the humans, even a train which ran through the park in good weather. A real gathering place for the two and four-legged beings. And the dog park was separated into large and small canines. I guess the city didn't want the small dogs preying upon the bigger ones. You've seen how the small ones just don't know how big they aren't. So, we did spend some time at the park, a few visits anyway, until we met up with someone whose dog wasn't in a friendly, networking kind of mood. Most of the time, Diego participated in mixing it up with the various breeds with the obligatory sniff and run; *catch me if you can*. We were cautious because while we knew of his kind nature and willingness to please, his look of being half lab and, particularly, the half German shepherd side of him challenged some dog owners and the dogs themselves. He never met anyone he couldn't or didn't like. And, while he was protective of his turf at home, he felt comfortable in this environment, being trustworthy of our judgment to place him there. Jesus, himself, never met anyone with whom he couldn't work. And he was in a lot of hostile environments during His walk on this Earth. But Jesus came into a challenging world, a world filled with antagonism toward the truth, a broken world with people who wanted to rule themselves, and others. We can take comfort in knowing from *John 15:18*, he says, *If the world hates you, know that it hated me before it hated you.* And from *Luke 8:36-37*: *And those who had seen it told them how the demon-possessed man had been healed. Then all the people of the surrounding country asked him to depart from them, for they were seized with great fear.* When we don't know the facts and don't have the information, aren't we likely to respond in anger, confusion, and summarily repulse those who don't think like we do?

Diego knew no enemies, just friends he hadn't met yet. Wasn't Christ the same, never giving in or giving up on someone? The story of the 100 sheep with one missing comes to mind. Wouldn't it have been easy to say a 1 percent loss is not so bad? *Not acceptable to His way of thinking.* We now reside within a short bicycle ride to a sheep farm. And never do I pass this farm without wanting to count and make certain they are all present in their field. God wants all to come to Him and be reconciled to live in glory and peace and union with Him. And yet even Christ knew when to dust off his sandals and leave a place, also chiding the disciples that if people chose not to listen, it was *their* choice. Dusting off your sandals can be a healthier move when they won't listen. We practiced what we'd learned after an incident at the dog park one day and never returned. If you talk with a dog trainer and they are honest, they will tell you to leave the dog at home for the first few lessons; it's the owners who need to be trained, building the correct mindset to lead the dog on the right path. My thought about this was reinforced after watching the owners of the aggressive dog and how their bullying attitude transferred clearly to their animal. It was a situation that was not going to be resolved with conversation, just an exit to safety. We *dusted off our sandals* and moved on, never to return.

Adam oversaw the animals in the original Garden of Eden, (possibly the first dog park), naming them all and utilizing each, to their strengths, for man's purpose. We have a similar responsibility to care for, feed and raise, in a respectable manner, the animals within our focus. **Genesis 1:28;** God tells humans to be good stewards of the animals, which includes taking care of their needs.

Q: I know you can find yourself in unperfect, hostile settings. And yet, while Jesus was able to work with anyone, He charged the disciples and us to "wipe our hands and shake the dust from our shoes" if people won't listen to His truth. We knew the dog park was no longer an option for us. The potential for harm seemed inevitable. What dust, places, or environments do you need to shake from your shoes, and move on? Most likely, it's your best move.

13

THE GREAT COMMUNICATOR

Throughout our life, we come across many people who we would consider to be good communicators. Whether that be in primary or secondary schools, churches, networking groups, civic organizations, or over the back fence. I've had a couple of those back-fence friends, and we could talk about a lot of something or nothing at all. And sometimes, that's the best kind of friend; one you can talk with and while they are not saying anything or speaking much, you can talk up a storm and feel better about the time invested. I have had varied conversations with my four-legged companions and they have been some of the best talks I've had with a being where we didn't exchange a single discernable word between us. Many of those meaningful conversations came in the last few months of Diego's life as he was in a struggle to walk and remain upright. To say those talks were tough is an understatement and were beyond my comprehension or ability to clearly think about the future, his, and mine.

But, as I have mentioned earlier, even a simple trip to the hardware store which took a grand total of thirty minutes, yet it must have seemed like days to ol' Diego. When I returned, a conversation would commence, and he would either scold me, deservedly so, or gleefully mention how he had warded off danger with serious intruders in the past half hour. "So proud of you. Good boy!" What may seem like days and days to our pets may be just a few minutes of time needed to accomplish a task, to be at work, or return from a trip. While there are tailless dogs, the Australian Shepherd being one, even without a tail he can wag his back end until he needs the doggie chiropractor. And is there such a thing? Of course, there are for all sorts of animals, dogs and horses included.

While the father in the following story, concerning the wayward son, did not have a tail to wag, he did everything else to show what his loved one meant to him when he returned. Read the story of the Prodigal Son in *Luke 15,* and I believe you'll appreciate the correlation to our pets. Our loved ones, whether they be human or animal, appreciate us and need us close. Having you, the owner, at home with your pet brings them comfort as well as it does for yourself. And just like the need to have our loved ones near us, our pets have the need also to be fulfilled. Connection cannot be overrated. Obviously, the father was connected and then disengaged for a period of time, anticipating the return of his son. The anticipation he must have felt, the waiting to see his son rise to his rightful senses must have been excruciating. And yet the joy experienced when the son returned, yet was out of sight, sent the father over the top. Not unlike the anxiety we feel, or pets may feel, as we wait for someone, or for something to occur. It's impossible to understand how exactly the pets in our charge experience anxiety, the waiting emotion, or the relief when we return. Simply know you matter to them, most likely more than you or I can ever comprehend.

One of my connections with Diego was our ability to communicate, and he was one of the most vocal pets I've encountered. The return trip from the hardware store was a mere precursor to the volumes of endless conversations we shared. I've been a trumpet player for quite some time and would enjoy practicing the music for the next performance, in whatever band or show, wherever and whenever possible. If I was simply working on a few lines of music, not particularly focused on sound quality, he would sit nearby and listen without offering critique or praise. And yet when the quality of the sound was important to achieve and I would hit a certain "ring" on a note, he was happy to oblige with some howls of his own, not because it was irritating to him but because he seemed to appreciate the music. His eyes would light up, and he would join right in. I don't believe he knew the tunes, but he seemed unashamed to lend his voice as a musical offering. With undeniable certainty I know he subscribed to the *make a joyful noise* platform of sharing his voice.

And yet, while making a joyful noise is a form of communication, active listening is a form of love. There are current campaigns on TV and other media that encourage parents and children to speak calmly and listen just as calmly to one another, creating communication we desperately need. You can speak to your pet. While they may not, technically, be able to understand your language or dialect, they will internalize the tone and caring voice they hear as something more precious to them than kibble. Praying with and for your pet will have results which may surprise you, but you do have to wait with a bit of patience for God to work through them.

Emergency vehicles were one of his favorite howls. Apparently, there was a 'ring' to the tone of the siren as it would pass the house, and he was happy to let us know when those vehicles approached, while smacking his lips in self-approval as if to say, "someone else is getting help; I got your back!"

Q: Listening can often be your best form of communicating. As you may have heard, it's the reason we have one mouth and two ears! When you don't have the words to comfort or express sympathy for those in need, you can listen, and they will tell you exactly what their needs are. Who needs a listening ear from you today?

14

THE GOLDEN RULE/S

The Golden Rule: No doubt established by the Golden Retriever Club of America at their founding in 1938. And, while they may claim name fame to the rule, this AKA club cannot claim what has become standard operating procedure for how we ought to treat each other. I do not think the golden dog has a lock on how or when to apply such behavior. However, some historians say the concept of treating each other with mutual respect dates back to Confucius or the Anglican priests and theologians of Britain who began using it as "rule or a law" as early as 1604. And as the Rule is worded, we are to treat others as we would have them treat us.

This implication that we'll respond to others the same way they care for us could be good and bad! The meaning here, I guess, is that we should wait until others act and then we treat them accordingly.

Really? God, what's your take on this idea? Can I or should I retaliate in kind, however I am treated? Just doesn't seem quite the way Christ took care of His flock. If I need to respond to the way others have treated me, then I may end up with a bloody nose, either figuratively or literally. Why should I wait to care for others or seek out their needs based upon how they have treated me today? Didn't the Lord, our Savior, go to where His people were struggling both physically and emotionally to seek and save? Did we do that for Him *before* he came to us? *1 Peter 4:8: Above all, keep loving one another earnestly, since love covers a multitude of sins.*

Good ol' Google to the rescue. When you want to look up *how to treat others*, a myriad of options appears. Google suggested forty plus bible verses. I reviewed a few, and how they might relate to our pets who seem to have the attitude of *serve first, then my treat will come,* without expectation of course. The Golden Rule states how we should treat others as we want them to treat us. It seems reasonable, but what if we take the initiative on how we want to be coddled, cared for, compassionately revered without a notion or expectation of how or what will be returned. It could just possibly flip the tables. *Matthew 7:12* says, *So whatever you wish others would do to you, do also to them, for this is the law of the Prophets.* Kind of swings the pendulum 180 degrees. By taking the initiative to engage, care for, listen to, and otherwise meet the other guys' needs first, we *arm them* with the knowledge and compassion that someone else really gets them, cares. **Galatians 5**: *only do not use your freedom as an opportunity for the flesh* (for yourself), *but through love serve one another.* You can look these up, as I did, and do the research, for there are dozens of ideas to cauterize this principle. But to emphasize my point, I'll give you one more from the original author's perspective. ***Ephesians 4:32,*** *Be kind to one another, tenderhearted, forgiving one another, as God in Christ (*through Christ's suffering and dying*) forgave you.*

You can train a pet to respond to a command in anticipation of a forthcoming treat. Likewise, you can train humans to do the same thing; literally the same thing, whether it be a job promotion, dinner out on the town for a spouse, or your child wanting a *treat* (called allowance) for a job done well. Our pets inherently do not expect something for something; they are simply bred for service. *Seasoned with life*, as I am, I have been around a great number of animals, many of them pets or animals put in my charge for the care and nurturing which is our God-given challenge and responsibility. And yet none of them communicated to me "if I do *this* for you, I'll expect *that* in return." It's a giving nature in its purest form and function. After reading this chapter it may be time for a little homework. Not the kind of homework taking a great deal of work, just a reflection on the pet experiences of your life and then noting how often those animals large and small have been placed in your charge while giving of themselves without expectation or want. Here are a few of mine to possibly jog some memories.

Over the course of time, I've had the blessing of memorable animals. Stormy, my original pup, playful and mischievous but kind to the end. He chose not to bite off my hand, as an 8-year-old, when he had his teeth around my wrist after he had been mortally wounded by another dog. He was simply protecting himself and in a great deal of pain and didn't want to be touched. Plenty of our cats have served us as great mousers. Their prize usually ended up on the front porch as a statement for us to observe. "Great job, Fluffy!" The equine breed of animal, those horses who just don't know how big they are, are ones who could crush or toss you with a sweep of their head. Their nature is to please with every pull of the rein, squeeze of the leg, or cluck to pick up the canter from a trot. If you're able to watch a horse and rider in the arena, pay close attention to the horse's ears. They swivel back and forth rapidly until getting a clear signal from the rider as to what their assignment is next, and then, like lasers, the ears pin forward. They don't have to listen, *but it's their nature*. Why should a 1200-pound horse pay attention to a 120-pound girl? Hate to repeat myself, *but it's in their nature!* It's inbred by the Creator for our benefit. Aren't we lucky!

Q: You may have already answered your own questions presented in this chapter, but I have another thought for you. Think about this...I've heard it said, "It's just a dumb animal." While I don't know who or what is the most brilliant being in the room, or in the pasture; I am well aware that if we don't learn from all of God's creatures, we're cheating ourselves out of knowing God better. What can we learn from their natural kindness toward us?

15

DEPENDABLE = TRUSTWORTHY

It is said that even a broken clock is right twice a day. Yet, dependability is in rare quantity today. Relying on the nightly news to reveal the latest scandal, the politicians who say they are serving their constituency, protests on every level and for every reason, and even the driver in front of us who won't drive the speed limit, determines for us there are very few things we can truly depend on. Wars and the threat of wars will be with us forever; and from *Matthew 24:6*; *wars will break out near and far, but don't panic...the end won't follow immediately. 7. The nations and kingdoms will proclaim war against each other...but this will only be the beginning of the horrors to come.* Yes, wars and hatred are certainly something we can count on because of the loathing and distaste man has for his fellow man. Wars are created within beings themselves, not from the weapons we wield, the missiles we launch, or territories we forcibly take. Yes, we can most assuredly depend on the human spirit to keep us in turmoil and at each other's throats for time infinitum. Unfortunately, there you are, all kinds of things we can hook our wagons to and count on to happen, again and again. A little sage advice is contained in a quote that goes like this: "If we keep doing the things we've always done, we'll keep getting the things we've always got." Got a clue who coined that one? Henry Ford said it. It was a reminder that people can get so busy with life, forget the sacrifice needed, and fail to include the small changes necessary to achieve the big results. A little more Henry Ford: "Coming together is a beginning, staying together is progress, and working together is success." Timeless advice.

I believe the words *dependable* and *trustworthy* are nearly interchangeable. It would be difficult to be someone who is trustworthy without also being dependable. From 1910 to today, the Boy Scouts of America lived by an oath, a promise, and the twelve points of the Scout Law. The first point of those twelve points is *trustworthy*. Check it out sometime. While it's not the Ten Commandments, those twelve *challenges* are a pretty fair set of guidelines upon which to live our lives. **Hebrews 13:8** says in the King James version...*Jesus Christ is the same yesterday, today, and forever.* The reason I mentioned the King James version is that in over fifty different versions I reviewed, they all say the very same thing. In the Jubilee Bible, JUB, it says...*Jesus Christ is the same yesterday, today and for all the ages.* Comforting to know that no matter how long we occupy this earth, our God will be here on the ready to take on anything we can throw His way. And by the way, the first point of the Girl Scout law is, *A Girl Scout's honor is to be trusted.* There you have it. If we can trust God to be and do as He says He will, and, in our secular world the Scouts can also be trusted, what else could we possibly need?

So often, we are not really sure what it is we need, and while we have a pretty good idea what we want, are the two really ever the same? The lessons learned from having a four-legged companion in my life for those nine years, filled my needs beyond what I could ever have imagined. Whether it was simply to have him close by, someone to talk and walk with, or to be responsible for, these are the things which come to mind without really knowing what my needs really were. He could depend on me to provide a bedtime snack as he went out for the evening. In turn, I could depend on him alerting me to an impending storm or intruders in the yard. Our pets are creatures of habit. Routines bring them comfort, peace, and stability. They are firmly set and look forward to repeating the same schedule today, tomorrow, and beyond.

The same yesterday, today, and forever. It has a familiar ring to it which constantly reminds us of the Creator of our world. *Psalm 146:6* speaks volumes when it says…*He is the Maker of heaven and earth, the sea, and everything in them— he remains faithful forever.* There is not a single doubt inhabiting my persona in which the spirit of God is not infused in our pets that we are blessed to care for! And nurturing these creatures is definitely in line with caring for the ones He points out when He says in *Matthew 25*…*Whatever you did for one of the least of these brothers and sisters of mine, you did for me.* In an article written by Kevin DeYoung in March of 2017 he says, "Likewise, it makes more sense to think Jesus is comparing service to fellow beings, with service to Him. Dependable, Trustworthy and Faithful."

Q: Who or what for you fits dependable, trustworthy, and faithful? How can we be **aware and alive with care** for those humans and creatures close to us? You may even be nudged to display compassion, understanding, empathy…but be careful, it could change your life.

DIEGO

16

FREEDOM

It is not difficult to live with the law; God's law as He designed it. It is actually quite freeing or liberating. Kind of like having a loving parent set a boundary and compassionately nudging us to stay within those set of fences. "But I need to set out on my own path, make my own rules and regs, and decide for myself what steps and courses of action are best for me!" *Danger: Trouble Ahead!* Knowing where the boundaries are, the *fence line*, whether it's only in the cerebellum or of the physical barbed-wire type, can really be quite helpful.

Galatians 5:13...*For you have been called to live in freedom;-not freedom to satisfy your sinful nature, but freedom to serve one another in love.* ***14...****For the whole law can be summed up in this one command: Love your neighbor as yourself.*

Loving someone involves more than the cursory warm-fuzzies we get when being near someone; but really devoting yourself to the person. And it doesn't have to mean simply human to human. As we've seen with our pets, the devotion they display and the dedication toward us is without compromise on their part, fully giving of themselves for our benefit, even to their detriment. In the final few days of my pet's life, he displayed compassion for me which I was only aware of after he passed. Since we were parked at a state campground, we were required to have our pets on a leash at all times. He had a thirty-foot tethered wingspan in which to work. And with this distance, he would literally space himself as far from the RV as he could go into the woods behind the camper. Thus, separating himself and his condition as far from me as his bonds would take him. He was devoted to the notion that if he could remove himself by any physical distance, he would then remove himself from the emotional strain under which I was about to experience. And I am certain if he was able to wander into the woods without that tether, he would have chosen his time to die, on his schedule; yes, and on his terms. How precisely similar is the love on display at the crucifixion when our Lord chose how and when to die. Even though He appeared to be under total control of the Romans, it was Him and His Father who had complete command of this situation. And how much more freeing can it be when you know the outcome, and the path you are taking has already been laid out for you. We simply must listen and respond with all of the prior approval we will ever need.

Galatians 5:1...So Christ has really set you free. Now make sure that you stay free, and don't get tied up again in slavery to the law. Referring to the Old Testament and how previous generations, 2000+ years ago. They were fixated on carrying out the law of Moses to the letter. Essentially penalizing themselves and forcing the doctrines, as they knew them, to rule at times without regard for the health and benefit of their fellow man. *Romans 5:20...God's law was given so that all people could see how sinful they were.* A really tough place to live when you know with certainty that you cannot live to the perfect standards laid out by generations before you. And *1 Corinthians 6:12...*You may say *"I am allowed to do anything."* But I reply, *"Not everything is good for you." And even though "I am allowed to do anything; I must not become a slave to any-thing."* The freedom to choose as I see fit sounds totally rational and reasonable to little 'ol me! However, healthy boundaries are a good thing! Devotion, loving without expectation, sharing our abundance and listening. These things and more are found in the freedom we discover living within God's law.

Q: As mentioned earlier, at the top of this chapter, there is freedom within the law. Knowing the boundaries, not those we establish as we feel it, but those laid for us can/do/will lead us down the correct path without stress or strain on our part. When someone else knows the route, and has the plan in place, why should we worry or be concerned about what we'll find along the way. ***Psalm 118:5*** *Out of my distress I called on the Lord; the Lord answered me and set me free.*

17

THE END IS NEAR

"Strong-willed this one," was the statement from the vet after administering the first of what should have been a lethal dose of medicine. Diego allowed the tech to shave his left forearm, not aware of what was about to happen next; or maybe he was aware and was yet prepared to accept his fate. Go ahead and draw any parallels you can muster with our Lord's final moments at the Crucifixion, and you'll see where I'm going with this. The words from the vet were in response to a nearly lifeless body, but a heartbeat that wouldn't, didn't, want to quit. It is normal to inject but one dose of serum to bring to a close the life of a pet; yet this one would not go down without one last regard for what he had been sent here to do...to comfort and bring peace for all those he encountered despite his final days in discomfort.

Philippians 4:7: And the peace of God, which

transcends all understanding, will guard your hearts and your minds in Christ Jesus. Unfortunately, I wasn't able to focus on the words of scripture I had learned while experiencing life, just on the terminal nature which was about to befall my long-time friend and companion. After a few moments, and at this point, time was lost on me; the vet offered up yet another dose which had its intended purpose of closing out the life of a family member.

It all happened very quickly, and yet I can still recall each and every second of the brief encounter we had in the vet's office. I'm not reporting anything new to those who have had the experience of putting down a family pet, but the longest and toughest part of my day was yet to come; leaving the office and driving home alone. In my case, I was based out of my motorhome during the summer of '13 as a campground host in a Missouri state park.

Deuteronomy 31:6: *Be strong and courageous. Do not be afraid or terrified because of them, for the Lord your God goes with you; he will never leave you nor forsake you.*

These are words I have/had to live by, not only in that immediate timeframe but for the years which have passed. And what I realized almost instantly, and has come to play a huge role in my life, is that I was not put here solely to bring comfort, joy, and peace to him/ Diego, but together to share our struggles in this journey. His/his role was to offer those things and so much more than I could ever conceive as possible. As I mentioned in opening words early in this manuscript, our Lord holds things from our conscious being; knowledge, understanding, and compassion from us until the time is right for us to comprehend and take action.

Certainly, I knew for the last six months of his life that he was in a state of decline and there was little treatment, medicines, or care I could give him to help or reverse the condition that took him. It was a condition that attacked his nervous system; kind of similar to Lou Gehrig's disease. During the few remaining weeks while he was around, we would attempt walks, without much success, due to his nervous system playing tricks on him. His front half seemed perfectly fine, but the back half had a mind of its own; almost like it wanted to lead the walk. He couldn't control the operation of a simple walk because he couldn't control the lower half of his body. And he would look at me with those big browns as if to ask, 'Why are we still doing this? I've taught you everything you need to know, you don't need me here any longer.'

Since I was stationed in a state park with other campers and animals, it was necessary to have him on a leash while outside the RV. And he would stretch the leash as far as it would go into the nearby woods hoping to relieve me of the pain which was about to happen; going off to die in peace on his terms. From **Jeremiah 8;** *even the stork knows her time.* Yet another indication is: *I will take the burden, it's not yours to carry.* Christ set the example as he separated himself from the others in the Garden of Gethsemane to pray and ask if there was a way that 'this cup' could pass. He knew His time was at hand and yet there was nothing He would do to stand in the way of the promise. Animals have an innate sense of what's right and the timing to fulfill it.

Meanwhile, back in the vet's office. After the

initial dose was given to Diego, he lowered his head with eyes closed and yet the heart was still a-beatin'. "We need to do the other side," the vet said. I thought, if this wasn't painful enough, we now must repeat it! But, oh dopey me, there are lessons to be learned and cherished despite my impatience with any job or procedure. Once injected, it was determined this one worked in the manner the vet had intended. Breaths are gone, and the heart is stilled. At which point, his eyelids open, the eyebrow flutters as if to wink and say, "It's finished, I'm home now." At this point, I am trying to fit my square thinking into the round hole of reality. Of course, I didn't want this to be the last time I would see or hear from my friend, but reality has set in, and we need to deal with it in the best way, the only real way that can bring comfort in the face of this loss. Rely on *His words and thoughts*, not mine.

"It turns out our pets have Last Wills before they die, but only known to the vets who put old and sick animals to sleep."- *Former veterinarian.*

A veterinarian was asked, what is the toughest part of your job, and without hesitation, he said it was the animal looking for its owner before going to sleep. Stats show that 90 percent of owners don't want to be in the room with their dying animal. People leave so they don't have to see their pet losing their life. But what the human doesn't realize is that in that moment the animal is looking for their owner, the person they need the most; their master to whom they have devoted a life, their very existence, for a good portion of time. Vets are asking owners to remain with their pets until the end. *It is inevitable they will die before you. Remember, you were the center of their lives, even if it's just a small portion of you; but they are a part of your family. Even when it's hard, don't give up on them.*

In the Don Bluth movie from 1989 *All Dogs go to Heaven*, a particular dog goes off to Heaven as a "bad actor." Yet he is sent back to Earth and given a second chance to redeem himself by helping a young girl. Nowhere is it written in the Bible animals will make it to Heaven; nothing specifically relates to their passage or that they will take up residence with us after this life. *However*, scholars and persons of religious nature, including Martin Luther, Billy Graham, and even Pope Francis concur the afterlife will be punctuated with animals of all kinds.

From an earthly reference...

In his book *Heaven*, Randy Alcorn writes, "Horses, cats, dogs, deer, dolphins, and squirrels— as well as the inanimate creation will be beneficiaries of Christ's death and resurrection. ...If we believe God is their Creator, for He loves us and them, He intends to restore His creatures from the bondage they experienced because of our sin, then we have biblical grounds for not only wanting but expecting to be with them again on the New Earth."

And divine references…

Genesis 9:12… And *God said, This is the sign of the covenant I am making between me and you and every living creature with you, a covenant for all generations to come.*

Ecclesiastes 3:18… *humans and animals have the same fate.* Solomon wrote three Old Testament books: Ecclesiastes, Proverbs, and Song of Songs. He is considered by many the smartest man who ever lived. If you're considering reading the Bible, that could be a great place to begin.

Isaiah 11:6-9: *The wolf will live with the lamb, the leopard will lie down with the goat, the calf and the lion and the yearling together; and a little child will lead them. The cow will feed with the bear, their young will lie down together, and the lion will eat straw like the ox. The infant will play near the cobra's den, and the young child will put its hand into the viper's nest. They will neither harm nor destroy on all my holy mountain, for the earth will be filled with the knowledge of the Lord as the waters cover the sea.*

Throughout Diego's life, his companionship continued to meet needs I never knew I had. We communicated on multiple levels, from play and exercise, through musical duets and the vocals he offered, to the verbal scoldings I received when I was gone too long. (Or maybe he was just filling me in on the latest happenings in the neighborhood which I had obviously missed). The most verbal pup I've ever known, compared to the one in our house now, with more on him later. Diego would share in good and glorious detail the events of his day, tail wagging with unmatched enthusiasm and always remind me, *"All is forgiven; where's my soccer ball?"*

Q: Whose burden do you need to bear, lighten? We must listen for those opportunities with both ears open. Who can you reach today with the intention of a singular, meaningful conversation? ***Galatians 6:2***: *Bear one another's burdens and so fulfill the law of Christ.*

18

MEEKNESS VS. WEAKNESS

These terms sound as though they may be interchangeable. Seemingly one in the same as to not even make the distinction between the two. And yet, as I attempt to explore their individual meanings and their relation to each other, my hope is you'll know and come to realize the power and place each one holds for us and our pets.

Perhaps you've heard *being meek is being weak.* Au contraire, my friend; they are quite different and altogether separate. As you have experienced in your life, I too have encountered times of each of the above to some degree. I can recall often and throughout my life the times when my abilities lacked enough strength or resolve to accomplish a task only to be overcome by the obstacle; the thinking that I just cannot figure it out, ending in the frustration which brings about hopelessness and despair. It's called *weakness*: the inability to fight back. And, if I rely on my own chutzpah to determine the correct path for whatever the issue may be, then I'm more than likely to miss the right turn on the road for redemption.

Do our pets show weakness, or meekness? Most domesticated animals have the fight-or-flight character trait interwoven into their genetics; they don't have to be taught. They are situationally driven. My wife and I have the blessing of living next door to our daughter's horse farm where we watch horses graze, riders learning how to jump the fences, and enjoy an occasional horse show. Most of these animals are of the thousand-pound-and-up variety. There is no need for weakness on their parts; no need to back down from any threat. They are powerful animals. And yet, they choose flight rather than fight. *Meekness on display is power, gentleness, and strength under control.* These horses have the ability to completely dominate their opponent and yet are inbred with the spirit of God. Meekness says "I have the power, but I choose to show my strength through restraint and dignity". Perhaps it was Diego's intelligence or the fight/flight mode to which he operated under, or even the meekness which kept him at bay by letting go of his need to protect his property from the coyotes, his domain. I'll never know. But *letting go* is one of the four areas of meekness that shows God is of the greatest importance in our lives. More on it later in this chapter.

And weakness vs. meekness is not necessarily a terrible or life-altering kind of permanent condition. Over and over the Apostle Paul proclaimed about his weaknesses so that God's strength would be revealed and glorified. From *2 Corinthians 11:30...I would rather boast about the things that show I am weak.* And further, in chapter 12, Jesus says...*My gracious favor is all you need. My power works best in your weakness.* Paul's response is, *I am quite content with my weaknesses, and with insults, hardships, persecutions, and calamities. For when I am weak, then I am strong.* What a paradox to attempt to sort out, it hurts just trying to rationalize it!

Fortunately, our pets don't have to. Once again, bred with the spirit God gave them of humility and service to others, showing not the weakness and despair as in us humans but the meekness of strength by submitting to the will and desires of someone else.

Weakness can be defined as "the state or condition of lacking strength, being at a disadvantage, being unable to resist, feebleness." References for this come from the Oxford Learner's Dictionary and Collins Dictionary. The origin of "weakness" can be traced back to the Proto-Indo-European root of "Weik," meaning "to bend."

If you've ever been through the job interview process, then you were probably asked the question, "So, what would you consider your strengths and your weaknesses?" "Well, boss, I don't really have any weaknesses but consider myself to be extremely humble." Oops, next candidate. Whether it's to a prospective employer, future mate, or a potential customer, we do not want to bring to light any of our own faults, weaknesses, or puniness. And yet, we all got 'em. So, admit it, move on and ask for help to overcome those moments, those times when we are weak or don't know what to say. See the plight of Moses in *Exodus 4.* Because, while we don't have super-human strength, the knowledge of all things or the intuition of Solomon, we do have *the* resource to draw from whenever needed; the phone line to God is always open. Make the call during those good times and during the rough ones in particular.

Diego had a shiny smile, or, some might say, a very gnarly or toothy kind of way of saying hello if you hadn't been properly introduced. If I were not at home, which was rare because I officed from the house, the delivery folks did not attempt to drop the package inside the door or the fence. "Nice doggy. I'll leave it out here." Meekness is a whole lot about knowing when to use it and when to back off while allowing others to shine. He was never mean or vicious, simply protective of the things in his charge.

In today's world, a meek and gentle spirit is often mistaken for weakness. We are to use our words, actions, and body language to exert power and force. "Take control," they say. A general on the battlefield, a coach of his college team never said, "Okay, men, we know we're meek, let's go get 'em." People often respond to fear. You can make almost anyone do almost anything you want when they have a fear of your size, demeanor, or delivery. However, is this the most effective behavior we should be displaying? Is this the side of us that Andrew Carnegie would say you could use to *Win Friends and Influence People*? If you can describe someone as a gentle spirit, soft-spoken and kind, they might be labeled as weak. But someone with those qualities can also be described as meek. *When we are meek, we have chosen to yield power and instead show compassion and gentleness for the benefit of others.* The Crucifixion comes to mind for me. How better to display meekness than to lay down one's life for another. The benefit to others without regard for His own skin was without measure.

When we digest Scripture daily, we should view it from the following angles:

-*What was God saying and to whom at the time?*

-*What did it mean?*

-*How does it apply to us today?*

The really nice part about the above three is their consistency from the time of the original text in the Old Testament until today. Nothing has changed; the ideas, ideals, and precepts all remain in place for us to apply what we know to our lives in our daily situations. God remains the same yesterday, today, and for all time.

The four concepts I came across relating to meekness are as follows, yet not limited just to our pets, as our lives are intertwined with theirs.

#1. Meekness means submitting to God. We bow before His word and will, recognizing there is no power we could possess on our own that does not come from Him.

#2. Meekness means we let go of our rights. *Privileges* and *our rights* are not greater than our calling as a child of God. We may become rich, famous, and influential, but He has so much more for us than these material items.

#3. In meekness, we see strength in patience. "But, God, I'm in a hurry, give me patience now." This is a tough one, and it may take many years of praying for patience in all situations to realize a state of mind to give us peace. Patience is strength. Being patient shows our reliance on Him who believes in us and trusts us to work in His kingdom, for His good. I recently read again a **Proverbs** verse which may correlate; *16:9...we* *can make our plans, but the Lord determines our steps.*

#4. In Meekness, we share the truth with love and grace…always being ready to share the source of our hope and shed light on our faith—a gentle strength that exudes power behind the gospel.

My best canine companion displayed and shared so many of these traits over his short nine years. I did nothing to teach or train these into him, and yet despite my influence, he excelled in the compassion and care departments. You surely have reflections on the pets within your own corner of the planet. Perhaps they are still with you and maybe not, but at any time and in all times we should give thanks for those that have crossed our lives and how we've benefitted from their existence.

Q: Being meek before God does not make you weak but makes you a disciple of truth, patience, and love for each other, whether it be person or pet. What relationships could benefit from you taking more of a stance of meekness? Who in your circle could use a measure of your patience and love?

19

APPROVAL

Aretha Franklin may have said it best when she belted out... "'R-E-S-P-E-C-T', find out what it means to me, R-E-S-P-E-C-T, take care TCB... I got to have a little respect!" She's looking for respect/approval and who isn't? A little recognition for the work, the effort and the time we put in to making it all work for good. Somehow, if I earn approval from my fellow man, then I'll earn his respect. Or maybe, if I receive the respect I'm looking for, the approval for what I've done will take place. Sounds like a complicated format and difficult to achieve. The person, group, or something I'm looking to find favor with may not be at all interested in offering such approval or may not even notice the *superior effort* I've put forth. Then, where does that leave me? Mostly feeling empty and without someone validating what I've done. "Look how great the manicured lawn looks after I mowed," for example. Or "Check out the shine on the Mustang after waxing." And, "Do you see the expertise that went into this project? There's some fine craftmanship there!" How much validation or approval do we need to be fulfilled or satisfied before moving on to the next thing, to say we're now *completed*. But know this: you are a complete individual, wonderfully made, just as God designed you, for and with purpose, without the need for human validation. From *Galatians 1:10...Am I trying to win the approval of human beings, or of God? Or am I trying to please people? If I were still trying to please people, I would not be a servant of Christ.*

There is a definition of approval, and it goes like this: the belief that someone or something is good or acceptable. –Britannica Dictionary.

I separated this to illustrate a point. The *human validation* environment is a very dangerous place to inhabit if I must rely on my fellow man for acceptance, for the respect that I believe I am owed, the approval for which I rightly deserve. Can the adoration from others ever be enough?

The approval of God is not earned but received. It does not come to you on the basis of merit but on the basis of mercy. Merit vs. Mercy.

"A life of ministry does not flow from an attempt

to win the approval of God. It flows from the joy of receiving the approval of God through Jesus Christ our Lord". Aug 16, 2020, Anonymous.

This is comforting, even exciting and very liberating, to know for certain that I am not held back by the need to be elevated by my fellow man. Our God has already lifted us to a level only He can accomplish and envision! Read *Matthew 10:32-33*...There is nothing wrong with seeking approval. However, we must be careful whose approval we seek. We follow Christ and the approval He prescribed for us. We seek His approval because He is our approval before the Father.

Diego, and all our pets, have a built-in need to be content within their environment while keeping their owners happy. As a dog parent I gave him charge of his domain, knowing he would protect and guard us as necessary. There are some small similarities between my approval of Diego's activities and that of our God who approves us without merit on our part. Without the preconceived notion our dog would perform to some level of my satisfaction, I simply enjoyed his attention and devotion. I believe God also enjoys our attention and devotion while giving us *choice* to choose our own path and forgiving us when we stray.

Romans 4:1 can be paraphrased…*Our faith will be regarded as the basis of our approval by God.* Working *for* approval is a never-ending struggle. Working *from* is liberating, just knowing that no other approval/ respect is needed by any person, place or thing.

Matthew 10:32-33…*Seek Christ's approval because he is the peoples approval before the Father.*

Q: Aretha Franklin's tune should resonate with all of us. If we're always striving for our neighbor's approval, a colleague's pat on the back, or a certain number of 'likes,' we are barking up the mystical tree which doesn't exist. It's given, not earned…you already have all the approval you'll ever need. Why stress and strain over something you already confidently possess? **Ephesians 3:12** *In Him and through faith in Him we may approach God with freedom and confidence.*

20

POSTLUDE

It's in the quiet, the calm, where we hear the loudest voices, those nudgings which motivate us to action. They are usually accompanied by an emotional response that moves our inner being to reflect and contemplate what our next action will be.

Over the years, I've had the benefit of listening to some great preachers with messages that promote calm, coolness of mind and spirit, charging us to unplug from the distractions of the day. Many mornings begin with a coffee on the porch next to my canine companion chewing on his favorite project; fortunately it's not my shoes this time. But the calm which flows from those moments provided by the new animal amongst us gives me the time and opportunity to quiet my soul and begin the day with the correct frame of mind.

As I close out this piece and move on with the current canine resident to occupy our house and our hearts, I would be remiss if I didn't offer some other resources, including the below-mentioned article as a reference and hope for you to consider. There are also movies available which you'll need to watch with a box of tissues close by. While sad and funny, they will always reveal something about our pets if we look at them with the eyes and heart needing something other than just entertainment value. Some of those movies include, *A Dog's Purpose*, followed by the sequel, *A Dog's Journey*. Another one you'll need the tissues for is *Marley and Me*. While it is sad when our pets don't outlive us, it is something to give us pause and reflect on a great representation of the love and sacrifice provided to us by our Lord. This is done without expectation or thought of their own benefit or even survival.

An article I read a short while back highlighted a dog which enhanced a family's life, not that dissimilar to Diego and how important and impactful he was for them.* I am in hopes you'll seek this out for another confirmation as to the value of our pets.

It has been over ten years since we have had a dog in our midst. Part of that being the current situation didn't allow the best environment for a new canine to grace our existence. The other part being, we were not emotionally ready to put our hearts through the roller coaster of bringing another family member into our home, knowing, once again we'd probably outlive this pet. And yet, I've read the studies and seen the results, and through personal observations, determined that it is a healthier and happier environment to have a pet in the house. So, when the situation presented itself to usher a dog back into the family, we did our research with various breeds to determine several behavioral characteristics, tendencies and good environments in which to house them. After personal visits with friends and family, and basically, overthinking the deal…we found a local breeder who had a beautiful six-month-old Australian Shepherd which was the last of his litter because he didn't have *the look* the other owners were looking for. Don't ever discount these *ugly ducklings* because they can turn out to be some of the most gorgeous swans you'll ever be privileged to know. He was a bit mangy at first glance and covered with ticks and burrs from the outdoor environment he previously lived in. And talk about nervous; he didn't want anything to do with leaving the breeder's car or coming home with us. But after many hours of brushing, plucking ticks, and making the vet appointment, he was ultimately set up for success in his new digs. He has become the most patient pet we've enjoyed. He allowed us to comb out the burrs, brush him daily and in turn, we tolerate the puppy which still exists for well, not sure how long this *stage* may last. You know the stage that says nearly everything within his purview is a chew toy. There are, of course from his perspective, undiscovered gems in the yard which he must uncover, (burrowing rodents, and the like) and the woodpile he unravels every day because it must be hiding varmints of various types; and *I need to rid them of their existence.* Yes, you are aware of this stage. As of this writing, he will turn eighteen months in a few days. But a great deal of thought has gone into obtaining our newest canine companion. A good deal of planning, care and nurturing to make certain our relationship is a good and lasting match. And God has done the same for us; matching us with our environment for best results to serve in His kingdom here on earth. ***Jeremiah 29:11:*** *For I know the plans I have for you,* declares the Lord, *plans to prosper you and not to harm you, plans to give you hope and a future.*

Ernest Hemingway once said: *In our darkest moments we don't need solutions or advice. What we yearn for is simple human connection* (or a pet connection in his case), *a quiet presence, a gentle touch. These small gestures are the anchors that hold us steady when life feels like too much. So, please don't try to fix me. Don't take on my pain or push away my shadows. Just sit beside me as I work through my own inner storms. Be the steady hand* (or paw) *I can reach for as I find my way.*

Your silent support is the most precious gift you can give. It's a love that helps me remember who I am, even when I forget.

Ernest Hemingway was a pet lover. He knew the value of having animals around, most likely a calming presence so he could pen some of his greatest works. He was known for saying he liked "nothing better than the feeling of having cats underfoot"; well, to the tune of around 150 cats between his Cuba and Key West, Florida homes.

In wrapping up, when we digest Scripture daily, we should again view it from the following angles:

-What was God saying, and to whom at the time?

-What did it mean to them?

-How does it apply to us today?

Pardon my redundancy from earlier, but nothing has changed; the ideas, ideals, and precepts all remain in place for us to apply what we know to our lives in our daily situations; those lived and learned through our pets. God remains the same yesterday, today, and for all time.

Our pets are some of God's greatest examples of completeness. They have their summer, winter, and raincoats with them, at all times, always at the ready. They don't need a vehicle, a social calendar, or a retirement plan. They possess hearing, sight, and a sense of smell we as humans can only dream about. They neither plan nor have an agenda that a committee needs to review. They just are! They are creatures God has given us to teach, care for, revere, and learn from. Very simple and powerful if we heed the signs. These animals, the domesticated kind, are curious and have the need to explore their surroundings. Any offerings you can make to enhance this innate nature of theirs will be to your pet's benefit and ultimately spill over for you.

Penning this work has been a cathartic exercise over the past years. Realizing the lessons learned, retained and utilized going forward will last for decades. Hearkening back to a different chapter of our lives (several years ago), to my previous Tae Kwon Do days, I was part of a physical testing to obtain a higher rank in the martial arts. We were required to write a piece on our experiences, lessons learned and the respect we have for our teachers and the discipline. I entitled mine, "Always a Student". Never did I feel too old or skilled to learn from those who had gone before me, studied under our Master, or had experiences I didn't. God's design for you includes the pet in your midst, the ones to love and learn from, and reflect it toward others. *Never stop learning!*

By the way, this new canine to grace our home and front porch is known as Clark W. Barkwold II, or just simply, Clark!

ABOUT THE AUTHOR

Writing this book, while an involved and daunting task, was not a difficult one. The love of the animals that I've surrounded myself with has been a blessing to be sure. Multiple dogs and cats, and some horses, have grown up with families intertwined from Nebraska to Kansas, California, and now in the Ozarks of southern Missouri. Our three kids and five grandkids have all shared in the raising and loving on the pets that we hold dear. While this is my debut novel, I will continue journaling about the animals that bring passion and purpose to our lives.

--D J PAYNE.

www.ingramcontent.com/pod-product-compliance
Lightning Source LLC
Chambersburg PA
CBHW060809050426
42449CB00008B/1608